Foreword

Imagine a teenager's brain; a fertile yet fragile expanse teeming with ideas, aspirations, questions and emotions. Imagine a classroom full of racing minds, scratching pens writing an endless stream of ideas and thoughts . . .

. . . Imagine your words in print reaching a wider audience. Imagine that maybe, just maybe, your words can make a difference. Strike a chord. Touch a life. Change the world. Imagine no more . . .

'I Have a Dream' is a series of poetry collections written by 11 to 18-year-olds from schools and colleges across the UK and overseas. Pupils were invited to send us their poems using the theme 'I Have a Dream'. Selected entries range from dreams they've experienced to childhood fantasies of stardom and wealth, through inspirational poems of their dreams for a better future and of people who have influenced and inspired their lives.

The series is a snapshot of who and what inspires, influences and enthuses young adults of today. It shows an insight into their hopes, dreams and aspirations of the future and displays how their dreams are an escape from the pressures of today's modern life. Young Writers are proud to present this anthology, which is truly inspired and sure to be an inspiration to all who read it.

Contents

St Richard's Catholic College, Bexhill on Sea

Megan Williams (14)	55
Matthew Hellyer (14)	56
Stephanie Myers (14)	57
Katie Leitch (14)	58
Conor Whyborne (14)	59
Alex Williamson-Persh (14)	60
Francesca Halligan (14)	61
Alex Moore (14)	62
Finn Donohue (11)	63
Laura Bradbury (12)	64
Laura Hall (12)	65
Alice Smith (12)	66
Danielle Doolan (12)	67
Conor Edwards (12)	68
Megan Francis (12)	69
Sophie Henson (12)	70
Victoria Turner (12)	71
Frankie Smith (12)	72
Colin Hamilton (12)	73
James Bradley (12)	74
Anna Rice (12)	75
Anna Hellett (12)	76
Melissa Carey (12)	77
Primrose Manning (14)	78
Anya Williams (14)	80
Sam Payne (14)	81
Lloyd Williams (14)	82
Kate Jasinksi (14)	83
Laura Green (14)	84
Victoria Cockerton (14)	85
Luke Bacon (14)	86
Jessica Perry (13)	87
Charlotte Rogers (13)	88
Esther Moorton (13)	89
Millie Gladwin (13)	90
George Potter (13)	91
Connor Blackwell-Foster (13)	92
Amber Muldoon (13)	93
Edward Dermody-Lawrence (13)	94
Hannah Moon (12)	95

West Hatch High School, Chigwell

Windsor School, Germany

The Poems

I Have A Dream

I have a dream that can only be seen,
by the mind's eye.
A dream filled with fiery passion.
that passion is mine.

I have a dream that only means
for the world to become one.
Together in friendship:
we are strong.

I have a dream that I believe
is a crime not to follow.
So take your most precious memory
and see how you love it so.

I have a dream and can proudly say
It's my world.
Your world.
The world of *today*.

Becky Brookson (11)
Arden School, Knowle

Can You Imagine?

Can you imagine
>That just beyond our world,
>Is universe upon universe,
>Yet to unfold?

Can you imagine
>A scream in the night,
>That piercing trill,
>Which would give such a fright?

Can you imagine
>The soft, sweet tune of a bird,
>Flying on the summer breeze,
>Just to be heard?

Can you imagine
>Looking to the sky,
>Seeing the impossible,
>A pig that can fly!

Can you imagine
>Speaking twelve other tongues,
>The experiences you'd have,
>And the languages you'd learn?

Can you imagine
>That in the years to come,
>Your head will shrink and shrink,
>Until it's the size of your thumb?

Can you imagine
>That in your dreams,
>Anything is possible . . .
>If you only believe . . . ?

Hannah Newby
Arden School, Knowle

If

If my skin were darker, would you treat me different?
If I were your copy, would you treat me the same?

If I was like you would I be better?
If I was your family would I still be lame?

If I had your religion could you accept me?
If I had your face would you like me more?

If I were a boy, would you see me unchanged?
If I were 30, would I be immature?

Do you judge me by gender?
Do you judge me by race?
Do you judge me by age
Or the look of my face?

If the world did not judge, would we all be the same
Or would we be different in many more ways?

Maybe you'd judge me by the choices I make.
Maybe you'd judge me by the way I behave.
You might even see me for who I am.
Now you see me through the eyes of Man.

If I saw you for you
And not anything else
Would you see me for me
Or like everyone else?

Hannah Brennan (13)
Bexley Grammar School, Welling

I Have A Dream

I have a dream;
A dream of love throughout the world.
Where wars are history,
Seen only in books and films.
Where abuse is seen only in the imagination,
The imagination of nightmares.

I have a dream;
A dream of love throughout the world.
Where murder is never true,
And only in books will it appear.
Where poverty is not heard of,
Unless parents tell of the horrors of the past.

I have a dream;
A dream of love throughout the world.
Where theft is not carried out,
Not even by those who need wealth the most.
Where prejudice is not a problem,
And is shown only in films.

I have a dream;
A dream of love throughout the world.
Where people are equal,
Where poverty is history,
Where people do not judge,
Where love is everywhere!

Beth Thomas (13)
Bexley Grammar School, Welling

I Have A Dream

I have a dream,
That one day the world will be free from wars,
God's precious world free from wars,
Fighting, guns, bombs all gone,
Just linking arms together, united.

I have a dream,
From Britain to Germany,
Churchill to Hitler,
The world will work as one,
Following Jesus Christ, the Son of God.

I have a dream,
Together we will work,
Enemies and foes,
All creed and colour,
To make our planet even more complete.

I have a dream,
That this may all come true,
The world living in pure peace and harmony,
Absolutely everyone together,
Forever and ever.

I have a dream.

Jack Bates (13)
Bexley Grammar School, Welling

I Have A Dream . . .

I have a dream . . .
I have a dream that every pet has a home,
An owner that will care for them,
A bed to snuggle in at night, on damp cold evenings,
And a feeling that they are safe and won't be abandoned
I have a dream today.

I wish . . .
I wish that every pet has food and comfort
That their owners are not cruel and treat them well,
And not leave them *alone* in the streets with no love and care,
I hope that every pet has exercise and they don't die of starvation.
I have a dream today.

Children dream of a pet for Christmas,
And don't realise that pets are a lot of work,
After a while people get bored and find new things to do,
Throwing away the poor pet that suffers,
Animals should be treated with the respect that they deserve,
I hope that in the future every pet has food and happiness,
And a wonderful healthy heart.
I have a dream today.
A good dream, a wonderful dream.
And a dream that needs to become true today.

Nicola Beeson (13)
Bexley Grammar School, Welling

Maybe Tomorrow

Maybe tomorrow
I'll wake up and the world will look a little different.
I'll look around
And notice everyone is smiling

Maybe tomorrow
I'll walk to school and see no litter
No cigarette stubs
No crisp packets or empty cans

Maybe tomorrow
The air that I breathe will be clean
No car fumes
No gas cloud hanging in the sky

Maybe tomorrow
I'll go to bed and the sky will be black
Not watery navy
And the stars will light up the sky

Maybe tomorrow
All these things will happen
And the world will be clean again
Maybe tomorrow
Maybe.

Lucy Bridge (13)
Bexley Grammar School, Welling

I Have A Dream

Wrongs will be made right
The horrors will be destroyed
We will live safe in our homes
We will not sit quietly

9/11 will be remembered
7/7 will be remembered
We will not be the victims again
We will not sit quietly

The world will be united
Different cultures living side by side
As one
We will not sit quietly

We will live in harmony
Without fear or mourning
A new day is dawning
We will not sit quietly

The future is bright
The future is safe
We will live our lives to their full
We will stand together.

Lee Dunmore (13)
Bexley Grammar School, Welling

I Have A Dream . . .

I have a dream that forever more animals won't be hurt,
I have a dream.
I have a dream that every animal will be man's best friend,
Maybe one day we will realise what cruelty they have suffered,
I have a dream.

I have a dream that all the little puppies and kittens
won't be abandoned,
I have a dream.
I have a dream that everyone will try and help these
defenceless creatures.
I have a dream that maybe one day, one day soon,
the world will realise what they have done.
I have a dream.

I have a dream that all cold-hearted people will be banished to a place
where no animal goes,
I have a dream.
I have a dream that no animal will be treated with such violence.

If only we cared . . .

Poppy Earl (13)
Bexley Grammar School, Welling

I Have A Dream . . .

I have a dream
I have a dream that one day,
Africa will stand up and climb over the bar
That is poverty.
I have a dream that one day,
We can be free of that weight and burden on our heads,
That is poverty.
I have a dream that one day,
We can all stand up without that burden,
Because we are all over the bar of poverty.
I believe that from north to south,
From east to west,
The weight of poverty can be banished to the deepest of depths,
Away from the human being,
And stay there,
Repelled by the good I want to bring.
You may not believe in miracles and that's OK for some,
But not for me.
I feel sorry for those who don't believe in miracles.
You should believe in miracles because we can make
                                        miracles happen.
Dream. Believe. Do.

Hugo Humphreys (13)
Bexley Grammar School, Welling

I Have A Dream

I have a dream that all nations rise in equality,
Which halts wars, hatred, greed and jealousy,

An equality which spreads riches to the poor,
And helps lighten up one's life once more,

An unbroken dream with broken lives,
But with unbroken love, struggle and strife,

On the other side of town brings you joy and greed,
That helps you drift through life with ease,

But let not the equator separate these two;
Let the love spread to the ones who need it too,

Let not the dividing oceans decide who we are;
But let us share our riches to poor places afar,

Let freedom ring in Kenya; poverty vanish in Somalia,
Place smiles on the faces of Brazil; shelters of love to Ethiopia,

Let us laugh, let us smile, let us spread these with doves,
Let us not hesitate, vacillate, let us express our love,

Like shoals of fish looking out for each other,
Like the sun and the stars twinkling together,

Let us rise in unison with peace in a family;
Together let us show respect to humanity.

Sulakshan Jayatharan (13)
Bexley Grammar School, Welling

I Have A Dream

I have a dream,
Of calmness and safety,
For the tested creatures,
The victims of our greed.

If the humans must keep,
Testing drugs on the beasts,
Then we must try to stop it,
And for them we must weep.

And while we live in good health,
We must spare a thought for them,
We must weep for them, cry for them,
And stop.

And to make them again whole,
There is much we must change,
For we are just like them,
Both one and the same.

And again we must think,
Of the ones we do kill,
Simply for ourselves,
We are selfish.

But why should we make them,
Suffer from our mistakes?
Because what we do to them,
Is just murder.

The creatures aren't beasts,
They are just like us,
Why should we think,
We are better than them?

I have a dream,
To help these,
The innocent beasts,
That we must save.

Joshua Lansdell (13)
Bexley Grammar School, Welling

I Have A Dream . . .

I have a dream that I can get my confidence back,
As well as my friends, my life, the positive thoughts in my head,
But I don't think that's going to be for a while,
So I'll stay here, alone, away from them.

I have a dream that I can stand up for myself,
To fight back and know that I did one better,
But for the moment that just seems a worthless dream,
So I'll stay here, alone, away from it.

I have a dream that I can walk around freely,
With a carefree giggle with my friends,
But at the moment the school toilets are the only place
They can't get to me,
So I'll stay here, alone, away from the thugs.

I have a dream that I can help those who are like me,
To stand up and speak out when they cannot,
But no one is here for me, so why bother?
So I'll stay here, alone, away from my fears.

I have a dream that I can make others aware,
That I'm a great friend to have,
That though I'm only one person, I still have value,
So maybe tomorrow I'll try making friends.

I have a dream that life will be bright,
Not black and white,
Not slow and prolonging,
Not hurtful or scary.

I have a dream that I'll get rid of my bullies.

Jessica Luton (13)
Bexley Grammar School, Welling

I Have A Dream . . .

I have a dream.
I have a dream that, in years to come,
Wars will be over;
People will live in peace.

I have a dream.
That people of different beliefs and nationalities,
Will join hands in harmony,
And peace will be in all their hearts.

I have a dream.
Death will be left to nature's work,
And weapons will be destroyed,
As will war zones and their damage.

We have a dream.
We can hold hands in peace,
No pain, no death,
We can make this dream come true.

Natasha McLellan (13)
Bexley Grammar School, Welling

I Have A Dream . . .

I have a dream
That animals are treated with the respect they deserve,
No cruelty, abuse or pain.
So they can be happy in life,
I want this dream to happen.

Little children dream of puppies or kittens,
But they don't understand the work involved.
To care and love them when they ask,
Instead they get bored and move on,
While the innocent animal suffers for no reason.
Why is this so?

I have a dream
That animals all have loving homes,
No animals will walk the streets at night,
Hungry, scared . . . alone!

Jockeys dream of perfect horses,
They do not care for horses that make mistakes,
Even if they offer their heart.
Horses give their trust to owners,
But are often let down.
Why is this so?

It's because owners do not know how it feels to have their trust broken,
Their homes destroyed,
Their lives shattered.
All for no reason.

Alexandra Smith (13)
Bexley Grammar School, Welling

I Have A Dream

I have a dream for the world's condition,
I have a dream that the polluted environments that we live in
will be utterly swept away . . .

Pollution whether it be noise or smell and sight should be defeated
And we should be able to live in a world with clear skies.

I have a dream that all the unclean streets in our world will be clean
And all of the trapped animals shall be free to roam where they please.

Please remember that even the smallest piece of rubbish that is thrown
down can strangle, choke
And even kill some small animals . . .
After all we should treat animals fairly,
They were put on this Earth with us.

But we can still live in a healthy environment . . .

There are plenty of opportunities and ways of helping ourselves and
others . . .
However they do not seem to assist very much . . .
I feel that if the way our world is today stays the same we will not
be around for much longer . . .

And I know that you parents out there have the dream of seeing your
children grow up and live rich, full lives.

So please follow these words said today and you could end up
without the risk of death early on in your life.

This is my dream.

Stanley Stewart
Bexley Grammar School, Welling

Dream Time

Everyone has a dream!
Dreams are wonderful things that transport
us to weird and exciting places!

I have a dream
I dream of shoes to wear to parties,
I dream of picnics and celebrations.

The child in America dreams of the new 4x4
his family are getting, and his trips to see
Mickey and friends.

The child in Turkey dreams of large
Christmas parties, tinsel and presents,
plenty to go around!

And the child in France dreams of the new white pony,
she's getting for her birthday.

But the child in Ethiopia
dreams . . . of rain.

Everyone has a dream.

Heather Thorn (13)
Bexley Grammar School, Welling

I Have A Dream . . . Olympic Champion

To become Olympic Champion is my dream
Oh, so I wish to be part of a winning team,
To achieve gold may be beyond my capability
But I will perform to the best of my ability.

Paula Radcliffe is my idol, a running sensation
A true hero and inspiration,
With strength, stamina and speed
She is always first to take the lead.

My wish is to be like her
An inspirational runner,
Putting myself to the test
To accomplish my dream and give my best.

Ramandeep Kaur (18)
Bradford Girls' Grammar School, Bradford

Do You Know Feelings?

Do you know how I feel today?
Can you see what's in my heart
Or hear what's on my mind?
When you look at the sky, what do you see?
Do you see an expanse of blue or something more?

Do you know how I'll feel tomorrow?
What will change and what will stay the same
Will it be like today?
Better or worse
How will you feel tomorrow?

Do you know how the crow feels as it flies about?
How about elephant, tiger or fox?
Maybe a water creature would be better
Like the dolphin, shark or crocodile.
Can insects feel?
Can they feel the hand that swats them or the foot that flattens them?

Do you know how I feel today?
Do you know how you feel?
Do you know how the homeless feel?
Everything has feelings whether they show them or not
Anger, happiness, sadness, they're all there
If you're willing to look deep enough.

Andrew Johns (18)
Chipping Campden School, Chipping Campden

I Have A Dream

I want everybody to know me and have lots of money
To spend on all my honeys 'cause everyone loves me.

Limos, jacuzzi, waiters and slaves
And they will work all the days just to please me
And make my life happy so I ain't so flappy and my teeth ain't gappy.

I'll live in a mansion with an OAP pension,
Don't forget to mention my millions.

This is my dream of me and my team and how I will be.
This is my dream, this is me, but only when I am 80.

Shane Blake (12)
Coln House Residential School, Fairford

This Is My Dream

I have a dream that everyone's dream can be seen on a big screen TV
to make it seen it would be a wonderful dream
because it could be seen by me.

I have a dream that everything can be seen not just by me
but by everyone, the blind, the people in different countries too.

My dream has been seen by everything and everyone
now let's go to sleep and dream some more.

No more can be seen but the common dream,
it can be seen by the dream team . . .

Aidan Cooper
Coln House Residential School, Fairford

My Ideal World

Many people dream of an ideal world,
They talk about what would be in it.
But when they're asked to help make it happen,
Nobody wants to start it.

In the world today you hear of fighting all around,
It's all you see in the news.
They said they were going to stop it,
But they don't have a clue.

But in my ideal world, there is peace and justice,
No guns or knives or drugs.
People live happily together,
Because of an end to the thugs.

In the world today you hear of global warming,
How it could bring an end to the world.
But through all the failed attempts to stop it,
We keep on getting closer to the end of the world.

But in my ideal world, there are water-powered cars, no gas or smoke,
It makes our world a lot healthier.
Also the ice caps stay frozen,
And that would be a change for the better.

In the world today we all know about poverty because of
poor schooling,
And how people are dying without hospitals.
Although our rich countries have done a few fundraisers
for the poorer countries,
That is only a little done.

But in my ideal world, there is no poverty,
Because everything is free.
There are also hospitals and schools for everyone,
So that they may have the same opportunities as you and me.

In the world, people spend too much time away at work,
Their kids hardly ever get to see them.
But when they are at home they tidy up or organise for the next day,
So the kids still don't spend time with them.

But in my ideal world no one has to work,
Or tidy or cook.
Robots are on hand for those jobs,
So that you can spend time with your kids, like reading them a book.

Warren Keymist (13)
First Light Education Plus, Chingford

My Dream Is My Wish

My dream is my wish!
I have a dream that . . .
One day the nation shall rise,
Rise together as one
To save millions of lives.

Many innocent souls
Need our help
The cancer victims,
The orphaned children
And the war-wounded,
Together we can add a few years
To a little girl's life.

Just two pounds a week
Can save a life or two,
Just running a mile
Can bring a smile,
You never know
What tomorrow brings.

This is my dream
I'm willing to make a difference
Are you?
My dream is my wish.

Thandeka Ndlovu (13)
First Light Education Plus, Chingford

I Have A Dream

Even though we're already the same
We all try to act the same,
Talk the same, be the same,
Yet I am singled out.

All I do is try to help
Yet they stubbornly refuse,
Their problems worsen, themselves to blame,
Once again I am singled out.

When alone with me they are normal,
We laugh and joke and chat,
Then when we reach the rest they change
And I am singled out.

I am a renegade to the others,
Cast away by the community,
I wander alone always trying to help
Because I am singled out.

I have a dream that we will be our own people
And not try to act the same
And I will be accepted by the people
Never again singled out.

Max Praquin (13)
First Light Education Plus, Chingford

I Have A Dream

I have a dream that violence will stop.
I have a dream that war will stop.
I have a dream
I have a dream
I have a dream that famine will disappear.
I have a dream that people will never become poor.
I have a dream
I have a dream
I have a dream that global warming will stop.
I have a dream that people stop littering.
I have a dream
I have a dream
I have a dream that we find a cure for sickness in this world.
I have a dream that crime will stop.
I have a dream
I have a dream
I have a dream that we grow more trees
And stop ruining animals' homes
I have a dream that animals and humans live in peace and
get together.

Shanice La Ronde (13)
First Light Education Plus, Chingford

I Have A Dream

Imagine a world with no violence,
Imagine a world with no pain.
Imagine a world with no anguish.
Where people are treated the same.

As I look out over the world each day
There's a number of things that I can say.
From the innocent killing of children too,
To poverty which is nothing new.

Imagine a world with no violence,
Imagine a world with no pain.
Imagine a world with no anguish,
Where people are treated the same.

Today people are judged by the colour of their skin,
Nobody bothers to find out what's within.
No one is able to speak their mind,
So instead they show anger instead of being kind.

Imagine a world with no violence,
Imagine a world with no pain.
Imagine a world with no anguish,
Where people are treated the same.

God created us all, so we can live as one.
So who has a right to kill with a gun?
I leave by saying I have a dream
And hopefully this will build up the world's self esteem.

Imagine a world with no violence,
Imagine a world with no pain.
Imagine a world with no anguish
Where people are treated the same.

Abigail Williams (14)
First Light Education Plus, Chingford

A Dream Of Peace

Dark cloudy night
Charcoal clouds
A piercing boom
A scream of confusion
A distressed mother
Ambulance, police cars, chaos.

I dream of a blue sky
A place of joy
A place of laughter
An open seashell hums in my ear
The shushing of the sea soothes me to sleep
In my dreams I have sweet dreams
I am smiling.

Anele Ndlovu (15)
First Light Education Plus, Chingford

Nobody Knows

I have a dream that nobody knows,
I have a dream of not wanting to let go.
I have a dream of finding my way,
I have a dream of having my say.

It's not much to want; it's not much to ask,
I live my life as if I'm wearing a mask.
Behind my smile is something you will never understand,
All I want is for you to take my hand,
Just to tell me I'll be fine.

I have a dream of not hiding away in fright,
I have a dream of sleeping all through the night.
I have a dream of leaving my tears behind,
I have a dream to have peace of mind.

What do I do to achieve my dream?
Will you listen as I scream?
Each piercing note brings hope,
Letting the pain leave with each tear.
I now know I've nothing to fear.

I will get my dream.

Hayley Kershaw (16)
Grafton School, Leeds

I Have A Dream

I have a dream that the clouds are clear of the dirty pollution
and the seas are empty of all filth.
I dream that there is fresh water in abundance for those
who need it most.
I dream of the ice caps not melting and
flooding the planet.
I dream that the rare animals of the Earth
will multiply.
I dream that people will share their treasures
with everyone.
I dream that there is no smoking and no crimes
being committed.
No disease, no weapons and
no selfishness.
I dream there are no wars and only peace
and happiness everywhere.

Liam Fox (12)
Heart of England School, Coventry

I Have A Dream

I have a dream that one day they will be proud of my achievements,
Where the future can only get better for everyone,
Where the world is full of happiness and smiles,
Where darkness turns to light and there are no regrets.

I have a dream that the past will not be forgotten,
Where there is no sadness, no crying, no emptiness,
Where children can live to their potential,
Where darkness turns to light and there are no regrets.

I have a dream that all wars will stop,
Where fighting will end by all countries,
Where the world is full of peace not sorrow,
Where darkness turns to light and there are no regrets.

That one day when they are proud of how I changed the world,
Is the day that I can say
The world is now full of light and there are no regrets.

Natalie Phipps (13)
Heart of England School, Coventry

They Have Been Here

Deserted children standing there, screaming, shouting to the sky,
not given a chance to say goodbye . . .
They have been here.
Parents searching everywhere
Wondering if they will ever place a kiss upon their
child's face again.
They have been here.
Houses burned beyond repair as the scent of death
spreads through the air.
The people left are just sitting in despair . . .
They have been here.
Traces lighting up the sky
As it is another person's turn to die.
People around, trying not to cry . . .
They have been here!

My dream is to put an end to this,
Let people who work in the army have a chance
of having a good life.
Give this Earth the love that is in my heart.

Bring back the love and peace to this world.

Yasmin Zahran (13)
Heart of England School, Coventry

I Want To Have

I want to have big green ears,
I want to have webbed feet,
I want to have four large eyes.

I want to live in darkness,
I want to wander in pure space,
I want to be feared
Yet I want to be harmless.

I want to be an alien!

But I am only human,
So I want to have a job.
I want to have a family
And two kids.
I want to live my life to the full,
I want to be myself
And nothing more.

Ed Roper (13)
Heart of England School, Coventry

Dreams

Dreams
We all have dreams,
To join the greatest football team,
Or maybe to do something extreme.

But this is my dream,
Not to surf the highest wave,
Or to explore a deep deep cave,
But to travel around the world.

But what will I do travelling around the world,
Maybe to see everything that is known,
Or to find anything and everything unknown
Or both.

But no,
To help endangered species is my goal,
Bengal tigers, the great ape,
I will hear the call of the lions and will have many narrow escapes.

What a cool, cool dream.

Joseph Dobson (13)
Heart of England School, Coventry

I Have A Dream

Moving to America is my dream
Joining the New York Yankee's team.
I'm leaving England to be a loner
In the canyons of Arizona.
I'm leaving England to get tanned
In Florida or California's Disneyland.
I'll have a wider choice of careers
But balance it out with a few beers.
I'd like to drive a brand new Lexus
After riding horses in the state of Texas.
I'd like to see actors like Bill Nighy
Or visit volcanoes in Hawaii.
I have a dream to visit Utah
I hope I do in the future.

Will Shaw (13)
Heart of England School, Coventry

I Have A Dream For The World,
A Dream for me . . .

I have a dream that happiness will fill the world,
Starving children and people in Africa will no longer be hungry,
Food, water and shelter will be provided,
Orphanages will find good homes for the homeless children.

Abusers will be punished for the misery they've caused,
Those who have done wrong will pay the price, people
shall be protected.

Love will guide us to a happy life,
Life will be lived to the full, we will stand by each other,
Love and protect
Peace shall be with us.

War shall stop. Health shall improve.
Tobacco and harmful drugs shall be destroyed.
Life will be longer . . .

Youths will stop vandalising and disrupting communities.
Robberies, guns and bombs will no longer be heard of.

I shall live a happy life and have a nice house.
I will fulfil all my dreams and respect everyone and everything
around me,
My friends and family will be there for me and I will be there for them
They will love me for who I am.
I will be individual and not follow the crowd.

You see *that* was *my* dream, my only dream,
A dream for the world, a dream for me.
No more, *no* less,
That was my dream . . .

Ellie Wynne (13)
Heart of England School, Coventry

I Have A Dream To Travel The World

I have a dream to travel the world,
Explore the land,
Help people and make them grand.
Dream the future and aim to be right,
Get your achievements and start to fight.
Travel the world to different stadiums to get my future
and win my races.

I have a dream to be a champion runner, famous
and proud of myself.
Collect my trophies, medals and certificates.

I have a dream to take over the world!
Just to make everything perfect.
Everything colourful, pretty and different.

I have a dream to travel the world.

Katy Wilkinson (13)
Heart of England School, Coventry

I Have A Dream

I have a dream of real pleasure,
I have a dream of finding true love,
But that dream is not sent to the skies above.

I have a dream of human rights equality,
I have a dream when everyone is somebody,
I have a dream of hunger being depleted,
And that's why my dream is of war being defeated.

I had a dream where racism was in the past,
I had a dream where we lived our lives fast,
I had a dream living in the future world,
I had a hope that hunger was being depleted.

I had a dream when my mind was positive,
I had a dream when my life despised the negative,
I had a dream when the world was full,
But now as I walk the streets, my heart hangs low
As I realise war can never be defeated.

James Frost (12)
Heart of England School, Coventry

I Had A Dream

I had a dream that child abuse was banned,
Children getting hurt was in the past.
That moment when this happened would last,
Children should be treated with respect.
It would be good to see an effect.
Would you hurt a poor innocent child,
Even if they play wild?
Why have children if you don't care
For the colour of their eyes or hair?
What do you get out of it,
Seeing them with black eyes and a thick lip?
Why bother wasting energy,
By making them your enemy!

Niomi Bohan (12)
Heart of England School, Coventry

My Dream

My dream - I wish . . .
The world is settled
Children have loving homes
Bright everywhere
Dogs having big bones
To become a famous rider
I want to ride a camel
I want to be a model
I want to swim the channel
I want a farm
I want a big family
I want a converted barn
I want a gentle man
I want to have a villa
In the heat
I want to have snow
I want to have a pool
I want to be an individual
I want to have money, but to earn it myself
That is my dream and my future is to succeed in this.

Bethany Lee (11)
Heart of England School, Coventry

My Dream

I had a dream, the dream was peaceful, tranquil and quiet,
No fights, no crime, not ending in a riot.
The world was blooming, the hungry became full
All was bright, all was happy, no sign of dull,
No punishment, no reason,
No death, no betrayal, no treason,
War became alliance, sad became gay.
Everyone equal in pay,
All equal, all fair,
Madness was rare.

RSPCA, NSPCC would not have to exist
Racism and abuse, hit hard with a fist
The drunks and the users
Were classed as abusers
Their slates wiped clean, their leaves turned over
The luck of the world, a four-leafed clover.

And I was my dream, the making of this
No boo or no hiss,
I was the saviour
Creating good behaviour.

The happily ever after,
Filling the world with laughter.

Alexander Shrewsbury (12)
Heart of England School, Coventry

I Have A Dream

I have a dream that fat people are slim, not fat
I have a dream that terrorists are no longer
I have a dream that racism is no more
I have a dream that bombings like 7/7 and
9/11 had never been done.
I have a dream that my family has a big forcefield
Round them and are never hurt or killed.

Bradley French (12)
Heart of England School, Coventry

I Have A Dream

I have a dream that everyone will be treated the same,
No matter what your appearance, your colour of skin,
hair colour, or weight.
You are you and everyone should like you for who you are
Not what you look like.

That there will be no such thing as war or violence,
No guns or bombs or knives
And everyone will be civil and treat each other kindly
Not violently and cruel.

There will be no homeless people begging on the streets
For money, just to survive.
No starving people in Africa and all over the world,
Walking miles for food and water.
There will be food and water, a home, a family.
Some happiness and a life.

No natural disasters killing hundreds of millions of innocent people,
No tsunamis, no hurricanes, volcanic eruptions or ice ages.
Everyone will learn to give to those who need it more.
Food, clothes, shoes, money.
Whatever it may be, there is always someone worse off than you.

People just wanting to be loved,
Many of us have everything, we should learn to love and help
One another, even if it's as simple as giving your spare change
To a charity.

Tobacco and drugs shall be banned, robberies and kidnappings,
words of the past.
People abusing children to pay for what they have done,
For all the pain and misery they have caused.

I have a dream that the world will be a better place for everyone
To get along in, the evil in the world be forgotten and a
thing of the past.
For kindness to be fulfilled and life to be happy and cheerful.

I have a dream that one day, maybe one day, it may come true.

Charlotte Miller (12)
Heart of England School, Coventry

I Have A Dream

I have a dream that I will rule the world,
In it an army of supernatural creatures will do my bidding.
I will enslave all of humanity and destroy those who oppose me.
I will be the greatest sorcerer in existence.
I will have ancient artefacts of incredible power that fuel
my destruction
I will wipe out all technology and make a life like the Ancient Brits had.
I will reward some of my loyalist followers with their heart's desire.
I will destroy any intolerance and any obsessed with hygiene
and privacy.
I would start a magic school and teach the most promising people.
If all goes well then there will be no negative things in life.
All of us will live in peace and harmony.
That would be my dream.
But I then wake up, that was my dream.

Ian Openshaw (12)
Heart of England School, Coventry

I Have A Dream

I have a dream about Sport Relief
To help Africa who don't have any beef.
So many people, so many poor,
That's why we all want to help them all.
Too many people, so many starving,
Lots of children in danger, carving.

They don't have water, nor food,
That's why we would visit them if we could.
Give money, give one pound.
Give some love that spreads around . . .
Run a mile in a team,
This is my dream.

Briege Letham (12)
Heart of England School, Coventry

I Had A Dream

I had a dream that animals were no longer treated badly,
That they were hardly ever hit.
Animals should be treated with respect,
Not be used for a bet.

I had a dream that animals won't be hurt,
Or kicked around in the dirt.
They shouldn't be left alone
Please give them a bone.

I had a dream that animals were no longer treated badly,
That they were hardly ever hit
Animals should be treated with respect,
Not used for a bet.

Why have dogs, if you don't care,
It doesn't matter if they have no hair.
Please men and women treat them well.
Don't give them living hell.

I had a dream.

George Wylde (12)
Heart of England School, Coventry

My Dream

I had a dream that the world was tranquil and quiet
Instead of the chaos that creates a riot.
I had a dream that all the war and fighting would cease,
All the abuse, neglect and slavery would decrease.

I had a dream that everyone was honest and equal
It was nice and it was peaceful
I had a dream that all the darkness and cruelty was eliminated,
That race and religion was not discriminated
I had a dream that everyone would join hands
Then there would be peace throughout the land.

Emma Lycett (12)
Heart of England School, Coventry

My Dream

My dream . . .
My dream is to help children have a better life.
Help children who are abandoned and left out on the streets at night,
By giving them a wealthy family and home.
For children who can't afford food or school uniforms.
I would help to pay for it and for the children in Africa
Dying of starvation and no shelter.
I would offer them food, drink and shelter.

Jana Harris (12)
Heart of England School, Coventry

I Have A Dream

That people can live in peace and harmony together
without being judged by their gender, religion or race.
In a safe secure place where children can play without abuse
getting in the way and religious faiths can worship freely!

Where all God's creatures, both big and small,
shall never be harmed, but left alone to roam and crawl!

Where greenhouse gasses are a thing of the past and
natural energy sources are here to last!

Where the west are made to share with their starving friends
and family on the dry African plains where the people could
die for want of rains.

This is my vision of a better world, where happiness is here to stay,
and there is no room for greed, just play!

Beckie Rayner (12)
Heart of England School, Coventry

I Have A Dream

Sometimes I wish that war could end,
Poverty over-ridden
Bullying beaten
And hate and evil banished.

That good was all that existed,
People were always nice,
The sun always shone
And everyone was always happy.

But then I think,
That the world would be unhappy if all bad were gone,
People would die and it would return,
No one would want to live in an unbalanced world.

So let it be balanced,
Because bad isn't evil,
And if we did not have bad,
Would we appreciate good?

Laura Blake (12)
Heart of England School, Coventry

I Have A Dream

I have a dream that terrorists didn't exist
That they faded into the mist
First the 9/11
Then the 7/7.

I have a dream of finding true love
Then soaring to the heavens above
I would rather true love be here
Instead of selling chips on Blackpool pier.

I have a dream of dying at home
Instead of nowhere all alone
With my family all around
Not on the streets, homeward bound.

Adam Miles Rubidge (12)
Heart of England School, Coventry

Demons And Dreams

Demons hang - your dark horizon -
Of pain and sorrow, lies and strife.
But you have wings - my little angel -
And you can steer your way through life.

Not wish nor prayer will help you here,
For on this quest you fly alone:
To craft and shape your own tomorrow,
And chisel out your path in stone.

Tempus Fugit - time's a flying -
The mists are fast descending in.
But be yourself and stand the weather;
And feel the glow, beneath your skin

Of change, rebirth, a new beginning,
Your future's under your control:
New life - new dreams - new things you're finding
You can change - and grasp - behold!

Yet
Unless you act upon your dreams
And take your future in your hand,
The mists will still come rolling in,
And in the dark, will demons hang.

Zarino Zappia (17)
King Edward VI College, Stourbridge

Fields Of Dreams

The land is embroidered with bright coloured patchwork,
The pieces all different shapes.
The colour flows over the edge of the paper,
The pattern flakes.

The prettiest patchwork I've ever seen
As light as a rainbow.
The brightest patchwork I've ever found,
Looking so yellow, it glows and this ground
Is my field of dreams.

Thomas White (12)
Marling School, Stroud

I Have A Dream

I had a dream of clouds gone by
when flying was mere instinct.
I had a dream of stars in sky,
disappearing in an instant.
But the dream I seek to tell you
lies beyond the unconscious line.
But a dream in mind for a future,
that will come back in time.
I dream to make a name, so that I will be renowned,
for when I die I hate to think my name will not be found.
In dreams are deeply hidden,
things, words just cannot tell.
It is a place where your soul is bidden,
someday all will be well.
We live in a world of poverty and violence
an unchangeable force.
But if perchance you dare to dream,
you'll take a different course.
I had a dream, I believed in it,
I called it my reality.
Don't call it superstition
a word that breaks it into frailty.
I had a dream that woke me up
to the world around me,
I had a dream, I saw the world
and it does not sleep soundly.

Alex Lagutova (14)
Moira House Girls' School, Eastbourne

Changing The World

Our world . . .
It should be perfect
it should be peaceful,
A place of kindness
where we're all equal.
So where are we going wrong?

World war is striking
down on us,
Conflict caused by religion,
faith and different communities.
Children crying,
Mothers dying.
Pain flooding our land.

Good to bad,
dark to light,
fire to ice.
A tiny candle in a dark room
is enough to change it from
dark to light from black to white.

So help me change the world today
and end this gloomy night.
Help me change the world today
and change this storm from wrong
to right.

Megan Williams (14)
St Richard's Catholic College, Bexhill on Sea

I Have A Nightmare

I have a nightmare,
That all lives are in poverty,
There is only the Third World
And no one has anywhere to live.

I have a nightmare,
That the world will be on fire,
That all lives are hell,
That all murderers will be murdered.

The world is empty,
There is no one left.
If I had a dream it wouldn't be like this.

Matthew Hellyer (14)
St Richard's Catholic College, Bexhill on Sea

I Had A Dream

I 'm inspired by people that help, like doctors

H elping people would change them and their world
A nd using what I know to help them
D ifficult time for you and me.

A bout the things that used to be

D ying everywhere but no one cares
R eally try to help out other people
E very day is precious
A nd knowing that I make a difference
M aking the world a better place.

Stephanie Myers (14)
St Richard's Catholic College, Bexhill on Sea

I Have A Dream

I have a dream, change my family
I have a dream, change the war
I have a dream, change my friends
I have a dream that my brothers are nice to others
I have a dream that people are happy all around the world
I have a dream that you can rest your head all night long
I have a dream that you have a dreamcatcher upon your wall
and the ceiling
I have a dream that the dreamcatcher makes you have a dream
that makes your dreams come true.

Katie Leitch (14)
St Richard's Catholic College, Bexhill on Sea

I Have A Dream

I have a dream
to run in the Olympics
to run like Justin Gatlin

I have a dream
to run for England
and for my family and friends

I have a dream
of glory and fame

I have a dream
to become the fastest
man on Earth

I have a dream
to be the best I can

I have a dream
that the world will be
a better place.

Conor Whyborne (14)
St Richard's Catholic College, Bexhill on Sea

My Dream World

I have a dream
that there will be no racism or prejudice in the world
and my kids will grow up in a successful job.
I hope they can grow up to be strong and give money to charity.
If they fall they shall get back up.
No robbery or racism.
Just think of a peaceful, innocent and positive thought.

Alex Williamson-Persh (14)
St Richard's Catholic College, Bexhill on Sea

A Vision For The Future

I have this vision of something great.
That all the skies are blue and green.
That the young boy helps the old woman across the road.
People are welcome from all walks of life.
In my vision all people are happy and helpful.
That makes the world so sweet.

But when I came away from this great vision,
I see a cold world which seeks to live happily.
Where the mighty are harming the small.
Everyone is miserable and sad.
This is what makes the world as it is.
This sadly is the real vision.

Francesca Halligan (14)
St Richard's Catholic College, Bexhill on Sea

I Have A Dream

I have a dream
Of my job in the future.
All the things I will have to do,
Hard or easy
It doesn't really matter.
You always get told
What to do.
I am still looking
Forward to it.
I know it is going to be
So much fun.

Alex Moore (14)
St Richard's Catholic College, Bexhill on Sea

I Have A Dream

I have a dream, my dream is this
to solve world hunger, bring joy and bliss!
I'll help the needy, save the poor
don't worry, in the end I'll find a cure.
I'll work until my dream becomes real
so that everyone may have a meal.
I'll conquer hate, stop all war
help those who need it, by opening the door.
The world at this moment is a big calamity
that's why my dreams should become reality.
To make the world a much better place
I'll give planet Earth a more caring face.

Finn Donohue (11)
St Richard's Catholic College, Bexhill on Sea

A Dream

A hope,
A vision,
A dream . . .

Of a waterfall flowing into a stream,
Birds singing in the drift of the breeze,
I'm swimming in water up to my knees,
One day I will go to a place like this . . .
I'll just disappear, disappear, disappear . . .

I have a hope,
I have a vision,
I have a dream . . .

Laura Bradbury (12)
St Richard's Catholic College, Bexhill on Sea

I Have A Dream

I have a dream, where we lived, in a world full of peace,
and kids were kids and adults' grumpiness would cease.
We'd all get along and never ever fight
and young people never see a bad sight.
A day would last for 32 hours and the sun would never go down
in each day no one would ever frown.
All people's fears would never come true
and have hearts full of kindness in all they do.
People would never go hungry or live another day being poor
and all their new lives they would all adore.
Children all had clothes and shoes for their feet
and no one lived in a dump on the streets.

So that was my dream, I hope it comes true,
maybe this year or in three thousand and two.

Laura Hall (12)
St Richard's Catholic College, Bexhill on Sea

I Have A Dream

I have a dream that
everywhere will be poverty free

I have a dream that
every human will be treated fairly

I have a dream that
everyone will have the same job opportunity

I have a dream that
everyone will help and support each other

I have dreamt a lot of things
but the way it's going none of this is going to happen!

We all need to do these things
to help save the world from becoming a war zone
for everyone!

Alice Smith (12)
St Richard's Catholic College, Bexhill on Sea

My Dream

I have eight dreams,
but to me it seems,
that only one is worth making reality.
The boy I like,
rides a motorbike,
he's tall, dark, handsome and dreamy.
This brown-eyed boy,
he brings me joy.
My dream is to make him love me,
I think I'm in love,
he's sent from above.
The angels have blessed me with bliss,
I'm on cloud nine,
the sun starts to shine
whenever I see him smiling.
The only problem is,
he'll never love me like this,
because I'm not the girl he wants . . .
this is one of my dreams,
out of the eight it seems,
the only one that is worth making reality!

Danielle Doolan (12)
St Richard's Catholic College, Bexhill on Sea

My Dream

I have a vision, I have a dream,
where everything's free, I know it's extreme,
but think of the people who have no money,
people from Africa, way over the sea,
these people could eat and not be hungry
and have the same leisure to share with you and me.
They could have baths and not have to smell
and lead a good life not a living hell.
Now I conclude my future dream
and hope it comes true, although it's extreme.

Conor Edwards (12)
St Richard's Catholic College, Bexhill on Sea

I Have A Dream

'Today was great!' I told my mum,
Even though I look really glum.
I want to tell her that my day was bad,
I want to tell her that I am sad.
I want to tell her that I feel alone
And that I only feel safe in the comfort of my home.
I want to tell her that they're after me
And that bullying me gives them glee.

It's getting too much, I can't take it,
I'm tired of being punched and hit.
I can't go to school, they'll come and get me,
Where can I go without being seen?
I need to run, right away from them,
Where will I go and when?
If I go they will hunt me down,
I'll have to live in a little dirt mound.

I wish that my dream would come true,
You're not being bullied, it's okay for you.
My dream isn't all about me,
I don't want to be selfish and take all the glee.
I just want all children to be treated fair,
Without living their lives in despair.
For no one to be bullied anymore,
There's nothing else that I'd like to ask for.

Megan Francis (12)
St Richard's Catholic College, Bexhill on Sea

I Had A Dream

I had a dream about litter
all flowing around the place
until it got so very high
it drowned the human race.

I dreamt about pollution
where the ozone layer died
and in the awful heatwave
the human race got fried.

I dreamt the ice caps melted
under the deep blue sea
it covered the whole entire land
it even drowned me.

I had a dream about weather
clashing storms and a windy night
even hailstones and lightning thrashed
as the weather was a dreadful sight.

I had a dream that the clouds were falling
and all you could see was complete white
it was getting very close to me
I've got to be honest it was a beautiful sight.

I had a dream about all of this
it was all very very true
these dreams are very scary
this might even happen to you.

Sophie Henson (12)
St Richard's Catholic College, Bexhill on Sea

I Have A Dream

I have a dream, a wish, a hope
Wondering what lies ahead
Sometimes I can't help my dream
And then tears begin to shed

I try so hard to achieve my dream
I work so hard and push
When I come quite close
It hides behind a bush

I'm not like other kids
Writing about the world and strife
No I'm totally different
I'm writing about *my* life

This dream it sounds so simple
But it's really hard and tough
I would like to be a wrestler
Yeah I know it's really rough

Dreams are hard to control
People hope they come true
Some people push themselves
You know that's me too

Let's just say; dreams I love so
Wishes I adore
Making them happen
I love even more.

Victoria Turner (12)
St Richard's Catholic College, Bexhill on Sea

United

I do have a dream,
That all men and women live,
Where children can eat.

I do have a dream,
That people treat you fairly,
Racism is banned.

I do have a dream,
Where people are united,
Nations are not at war.

I do have a dream,
When we live long lives of good,
I do have a dream.

I don't want to see,
When people kill their own race,
For the victim's race.

I don't want to see,
Bombs raining down all over,
People's lives at risk.

I don't want to see,
Kids' dreams crushed by others,
I don't want to see.

I do have a dream,
With peace over all nations,
I do have a dream.

Frankie Smith (12)
St Richard's Catholic College, Bexhill on Sea

I Have A Dream

In the future this could happen
people in Africa will not suffer
it is not fair on them.

This is not their own fault
every day a child and adult starves
oh my god this should not have happened.

All these people should dream for this
for all this to happen
they don't even have a football team

Even if they did they could still suffer
hopefully this can change
thank you for listening to my dream.

Colin Hamilton (12)
St Richard's Catholic College, Bexhill on Sea

I Have A Dream

I have a dream . . .

That there will be no wars
There will be no suffering

That everyone has money
That everyone has food and water

That everyone has a home
That everyone is treated fairly

That there are no slaves
That there is world peace

That we can get along
That there are no more crimes

That nobody is discriminated against
That nobody is hated

I have a dream . . .
That dreams come true.

James Bradley (12)
St Richard's Catholic College, Bexhill on Sea

I Had A Dream

I had a dream the other night
I had a dream in my sleep
A dream of amazing blinding light
A dream that made me weep.

In my dream I saw a man
I saw a woman too
He held in his hand a begging can
They had nothing else to do.

So I thought about my dream
I wondered what it meant
Then I knew from that moment
That's how my life would be spent.

I'd go and help these poor people
Who have nothing at all to eat
I'll give them water to drink
Now my destiny I must go meet.

Anna Rice (12)
St Richard's Catholic College, Bexhill on Sea

I Have A Dream

I have a dream each night
When I lay asleep in my bed
I think how full up I am
And wish everyone could be fed

I stretch and yawn on my pillow
And pull open the curtains wide
I stare at the stars up above
And dream of all those who've died

When I wake up, I put on my clothes
And try to look my best
I feel the soft warm fabric
And wish everyone could be dressed.

When I arrive at school
And meet with everyone
My friends greet me and I wish
That all had a friend in someone.

So that is my dream
I hope that one day
It will all happen
As I dream it and pray.

Anna Hellett (12)
St Richard's Catholic College, Bexhill on Sea

My Dream

I have a dream of love and hope,
For all of humankind.

Let people know how lucky they are
And let them bear it in mind.

Although this dream is hard to succeed,
I still try to prove my reason.

People just take no notice and walk,
Whatever the day or season.

Even though many people may walk,
It has been so important to me.

I'll never give up my dream,
Whenever the place or time may be.

Melissa Carey (12)
St Richard's Catholic College, Bexhill on Sea

Can You See A World?

Can you see a world,
Without any harm,
A world that's happy,
Where angry is calm?

Can you see a world,
Where there's no fighting,
A world with no fear,
Where there's no swearing?

Can you see a world
Where nobody cries,
A world that's honest,
Without any lies?

Can you see a world,
Where war is no more,
A world that's equal,
With peace at its core?

Can you see a world,
Where no one is hated,
A world that is kind,
With peace celebrated?

Can you see a world,
Where everyone cheers,
A world full of smiles,
Without any tears?

Can you see a world,
Where harmony rules,
A world with no crime,
Where convicts are fools?

Can you see a world,
A short time from now,
A world that is good,
Happiness, but how?

Can you see a world,
World peace at long last,
A world that can be?
Let's make war the past.

Primrose Manning (14)
St Richard's Catholic College, Bexhill on Sea

Peace

Peace is when they've all gone out
When the phone just doesn't ring,
Peace is time all to myself
Private time to hum and sing.

Peace is when the people don't argue
When police aren't ever called out,
Peace is when the drunk stay sober
And the murderers are never about.

Peace is when they ban all guns
When everyone is forgiven and sorry,
Peace is when the wars are over
No reason to fret or worry.

Anya Williams (14)
St Richard's Catholic College, Bexhill on Sea

I Have A Dream

The world will be good,
People acting like they should.
Instead of being bad,
They should be very glad.

The world will be content,
Instead of being bent.
People should enjoy what they've got,
Instead of fighting for what they've not.

The world will be full of happy faces,
No matter what people's religion or races.
Who cares what people believe,
Is this a cause to bully and thieve?

The world will be a place full of fun,
The people united, together as one.
Everyone will be happy instead of down,
Nobody will ever have cause to frown.

Sam Payne (14)
St Richard's Catholic College, Bexhill on Sea

Dream

Dream, dream, dream,
The dream is peace, peace, peace
We need to help.

We need to give, give, give,
They deserve the same life.

We need to stop, stop, stop the war,
Because they need peace.
They need help, help, help,
So give them what you can.

Do yourself proud, proud, proud
And help
Their life, life, life
Is in your hands!

Lloyd Williams (14)
St Richard's Catholic College, Bexhill on Sea

I Have A Dream

I dream a life that's great and good
So that I'm happy all the time
I dream a life that's happy and fulfilling
Please help, I need a sign.

I dream of health that's long and fine
So I can live to see the day
I dream of health that's sweet and happy
For when I relax before the bay.

I dream of spirit that's free and flowing
So I can breathe in and out
I dream of spirit that's alive and awake
For when I'm running about.

I dream a life that's great and good
So that I'm happy all the time
I dream a life that's happy and fulfilling
Please help, I need a sign.

Kate Jasinksi (14)
St Richard's Catholic College, Bexhill on Sea

I Have A Dream

I have a dream, about peace in our time,
About love in our world, in a world without crime,
No more death, no more tears, no more crying, no more fears,
No more bombs, no more suffering to scream in our ears.

I have a dream, about war that is gone,
About friendship and trust and a light that is shone
A light that displays an unwavering love,
A gift that will shine from the heavens above.

I have a dream, about peace in our time,
A life full of love, a life that is mine,
A love unconditional, acceptance that's true,
This my Lord comes from the whole that is You.

Laura Green (14)
St Richard's Catholic College, Bexhill on Sea

Do You Dream As I Dream?

Do you dream as I dream
For life to be fair?

Do you dream as I dream
For no theft or greed?

Do you dream as I dream
For no pollution?

Do you dream as I dream
To live a healthy life?

Do you dream as I dream
For equality?

Do you dream as I dream
For everlasting happiness?

Do you dream as I dream
For no illness or pain?

Do you dream as I dream
For free life?

Dream as I dream
To be with others forever.

Dream as I dream
And we can endeavour.

Victoria Cockerton (14)
St Richard's Catholic College, Bexhill on Sea

Imagine

Peace is when everyone has enough food,
And all the rich countries don't intrude.
One day everyone will have homes,
Then there will be no need to moan.

Perfect is when it is a nice sunny day,
And everyone will not have to pay.
Everyone needs to have happiness,
Otherwise they will be filled with madness.

Imagine a world without global warming,
Then there will be no more thawing.
Sadness is when there is no hope left,
Injustice in the world comes to a head.

Tomorrow will always be finer,
Then everyone will look forward to better.
Maybe one day we will be perfect,
And not have to worry about our defect.

One day maybe all of this will be real,
Until that comes we will still be surreal.
Hope is something we will always have,
It is certain someone will always grab.

Luke Bacon (14)
St Richard's Catholic College, Bexhill on Sea

I Have A Dream

I have a dream that . . .
We will respect each other, every day,
And treat each other equally in every single way!

I have a dream that . . .
Everybody will judge each other the same,
Even if their skin colour's different, or they have a funny name!

I have a dream that . . .
There could be a better future, for you and me,
If we all respect each other equally, we have a chance to see!

I have a dream that . . .
All the children in the world, both black and white,
Will join their hands together, that, I think is right!

Jessica Perry (13)
St Richard's Catholic College, Bexhill on Sea

I Have A Dream!

I have a dream that . . .
there's a better future for me and you,
that all races stick together like glue.

I have a dream that . . .
everyone sees God's light,
that everyone tucks into a feast at night.

I have a dream that . . .
there will be no racism
and Africa gets clean water on a daily basis.

I have a dream that . . .
all the countries have good health
and all the countries have good wealth.

I have a dream that . . .
there will be no STIs and HIV
so everyone can live disease free.

I have a dream that . . .
everyone will have a nice home,
and be grateful and not moan.

I have a dream that . . .
everyone is filled with laughter,
and finally I wish everyone lives happily ever after!

I have a dream!

Charlotte Rogers (13)
St Richard's Catholic College, Bexhill on Sea

I Have A Dream

I've dreamt of something better than this,
A perfect life just for me,
Without being racist or prejudice or sexist,
How great then would life be?

I wished that we could be friends,
No fighting or wars just peace.
I wished that one day we could be happy
And I wished all the bad things would cease.

I'd hoped that we were past all this,
The insults and the swearing,
But maybe you haven't grown up yet,
You used to be kind and caring.

I've dreamt of something better than this,
A life made of love, hope and care,
A life where everyone is equal,
A life that we can all share.

Esther Moorton (13)
St Richard's Catholic College, Bexhill on Sea

Wouldn't It Be Nice . . .

Wouldn't it be nice . . .
If everyone got along?
That's not happening.

Wouldn't it be nice . . .
If people stopped all the wars?
That's not happening.

Wouldn't it be nice . . .
If illnesses were cured?
That's not happening.

Wouldn't it be nice . . .
If all children went to school?
That's not happening.

Wouldn't it be nice . . .
If all these things became true?
All of us can try.

Millie Gladwin (13)
St Richard's Catholic College, Bexhill on Sea

I Have A Dream

I have a dream
for a better future
instead of torture.

I have a dream
to be a rugby star,
not to work in a pub bar.

I have a dream
about my mum and dad
about what they once had.

I have a dream
to be like Robinho
or like Ronaldinho.

I have a dream
there is only one race,
human race.

George Potter (13)
St Richard's Catholic College, Bexhill on Sea

Aims

Aim
To be able to stand up for myself.

Aim
To be able to achieve what I want to achieve.

Aim
To be good to everyone I meet.

Aim
To make the world a better place.

Aim
To be able to stand up against bullying.

Aims
These are what I want to achieve.

Connor Blackwell-Foster (13)
St Richard's Catholic College, Bexhill on Sea

I Have A Dream

I have a dream that we all live in peace,
I have a dream world hunger wouldn't be,
I have a dream we wouldn't judge by what we see,
I have a dream there will be no more war,
I have a dream that we could find the cure,
I have a dream no innocent would die,
I have a dream there'd be no more lies,
I have a dream we'll all be friends,
I have a dream we'd live in hope,
I have a dream we will stick together in the end.
I have a dream!

Amber Muldoon (13)
St Richard's Catholic College, Bexhill on Sea

I Have A Dream

I have a dream
To have a better future for me and you.
I have had a thought
To share the world's resources.
I have had some knowledge
To receive the Earth's inventions.
I have received communications
To not give up, to stop war.
I have heard from my prayers
To take in the colours of the world.
I have listened from the gods
To retreat the power and destruction.
I have the sign
To live in a world of a wise evolution.

Edward Dermody-Lawrence (13)
St Richard's Catholic College, Bexhill on Sea

I Have A Dream

I have a dream
That racism and discrimination
Are done away with.

I have a dream
That fair trade will become worldwide
And those who slave for the good of the world
Get what they deserve.

I have a dream
That war will become a thing of the past
And that all countries, races, religions
And cultures will live together in peace and unity.

It doesn't matter what colour you are
Or what faith you have,
It's what is inside that counts.

Hannah Moon (12)
St Richard's Catholic College, Bexhill on Sea

Emptiness

If we all had no possessions,
We'd have nothing more to gain,
Nothing more to achieve,
Nothing more to want,
Nothing to set anyone apart
Or make them more important,
No rich, no poor, no wrong, no right,
Equality.
No need for greed, no need to fight,
The only weapons being words,
No gods, no beliefs, no prejudice,
No upper class, no slaves,
No knowledge, no power,
No exams, no grades,
Nothing.
A future?
If we have nothing, if we know nothing,
We have everything,
We have unity,
We have peace.

Emily Vine (13)
St Richard's Catholic College, Bexhill on Sea

I Have A Dream

I have a dream that we can all stop littering,
So we can live in a cleaner world.

Where birds fly freely in the sky,
Instead of on the ground strangled by a plastic beer ring.

Where rivers are clear, clean and fresh
Instead of dirty and polluted.

Where children can go out and play
Instead of having to go in because of litter and rats.

If we clean up our world before it's too late,
Everyone will be happy! You decide our fate.

Amy Townson (13)
St Richard's Catholic College, Bexhill on Sea

I Have A Dream

I have a dream of glory
No one has a reason to be sorry
There will be no need to shed a tear
No need to live in a world of fear
There is no room for sorrow
I have a dream the world would change tomorrow
I have a dream there is no pain
There is no reason for tears of rain
I have a dream of happiness
The poor won't have to live like this
I have a dream of freedom
I have a dream there is no poor
I have a dream of so much more
That there is no racism
Everyone lives with happiness
No one has a reason to fight
There is no dark but light
Whatever you wear
Whatever you look like
You are who you are
Let no one change you
There is no need of feeling blue
I have a dream of freedom and equality
I have a dream of happiness and glamour
I have a dream there is no sorrow
I have a dream the world would change tomorrow.

Nikita Hilton (13)
St Richard's Catholic College, Bexhill on Sea

I Have A Dream

I have a dream,
That everyone lives in peace
And people understand and respect others.
I have a dream,
That no one has to experience loss caused by another person.
I have a dream,
That the less educated are given a chance
And can be helped to achieve their dreams,
Just the same as everyone else.
I have a dream,
That no matter the colour of skin
Everyone is treated in a kind and loving way.

Tom Knapp (13)
St Richard's Catholic College, Bexhill on Sea

I Have A Dream

I have a dream
That animals can live
Without the fear of humans.

I have a dream
That family matters the most
With Sunday roast and a Christmas meal,
Let's have something to toast.

I have a dream
That Africa has food,
That poverty does not exist
And helps them change their mood.

I have a dream
That bullies are no more,
Schools can be a happy place
When you walk through the door.

I have a dream
That the world has peace,
No bombs, no war, no anything
And slaves can be released.

Lauren Brightiff (13)
St Richard's Catholic College, Bexhill on Sea

A Friend Like You!

(Inspired by a famous poem)

'Written with a pen,
Sealed with a kiss,
If you're my friend answer me this,
Are you kind or are you not?
You told me once but I forgot.'
You've helped me through a lot of things,
And given me my angel wings,
I'm happy to know
A friend,
Be a friend
And love a friend like you!

Jess Bennett (12)
The Hayfield School, Auckley

In A Dream I Walk With You

I dream a lot,
I always do
And when I do, I dream of you.
I dream of peace around the world,
No fights, no war, no pain.
I dream of happy thoughts of you,
In a dream together, me and you.
I dream the world will show the rain
And make me see a rainbow.
I dream the sun will shine again
And follow me wherever I go.

Anne Haas (14)
The Hayfield School, Auckley

I Have A Dream

I have a dream,
This one did not make me scream,
This was a nice dream about Rooney,
A great footballer who gives fans glory.

Rooney inspires me
But he has a bad temper doesn't he?
He can pass, he can score,
Please Rooney score one more.
Rooney play well for your team,
Thank you for being in my dream.

Daniel Payne (12)
The Hayfield School, Auckley

I Wish . . .

I wish I was a tiger
Running in the sun.
I wish I was a leopard
Pouncing and having fun.

I wish I was a dolphin
Swimming in the deep blue ocean.
I wish I was a tortoise
Always going in slow motion.

I wish I was a raging dog
Covered with lots of hair.
I wish I was a centipede
With plenty of legs to spare.

There are lots of things
That I want to be,
But the best thing I am good at
Is being me!

Alex Bass (12)
The Hayfield School, Auckley

I Keep Changing My Mind

At the minute changing my mind seems to be a hobby,
When I was 5 the only person I looked up to
Was my favourite person, Noddy.
Years later I changed my mind again to someone very special
And in their peak of fame.
But at the minute my mind seems to have broken down
Because no one seems to inspire me.
Well no one who I have found.

Annabel Upton (12)
The Hayfield School, Auckley

Something

I have a dream for the whole world to get along,
No hatred, no wars, no global warming, no bombs,
I want there to be peace,
Bob Geldof thinks the same things as me.

Some people talk in magazines, in the press and on the telly.
But only Sir Bob did something indefinitely.
He did something, changed something, made something.
How many people can say, 'I saved 1,000 people, yeh that was me.'

Lauren Pask (12)
The Hayfield School, Auckley

I Had A Dream, Where Has It Gone?

A futuristic world
Where black and white mix.
Euros are in England
And everyone is rich.

Cars that change to aeroplanes
And what are mobile phones?
All that's used is hands-free now,
A world we do not know.

Where are all the three wheeled cars
And the town street beggars?
All the things I thought were safe
Have gone, stolen.

All these gadgets, games and toys
Can and are a bonus,
But where is love and happiness?
All forgotten and gone.

Children's laughter and adults chatting
All now looked upon in shame.
What to think? What to do?
Where am I?

Jenni Hanford (12)
The Hayfield School, Auckley

Impossible Dream

I had a dream of my future days,
And how life had changed in different ways.
Only a few years had gone past
But I was feeling better at last.
More bright thoughts were there with me,
I was heading where I wanted to be.

I was helping people which suffered sadly,
They needed someone to share with, badly.
I was finally up there trying, but admired,
Trying not to slip, to go back and be tired.
I was not in it for money or wealth,
But I had found a cure for mental health.

So when I finally woke and thought what to do,
To make my impossible dream come true.

Lucy House (13)
The Hayfield School, Auckley

Flashback To The Future!

This has been a dream of mine -
That my near future will shine
Of innocence from the past,
So 1900 would come and last.

Children chanted, clapped and sang,
Quarrels without bombs or bangs.
Music was a proper art -
A creation to move the heart.

Technology was never pined,
Just a help to our mankind.
Why is life all price tagged now?
All cheesy ads to make you go, 'Wow!'

If the distant dream of mine
Could come true, my life will shine.
A future of innocence from the past,
Back to the future, I hope will last.

Lucy Warnock (12)
The Hayfield School, Auckley

I Have A Dream

I have a dream, a dream to be a vet or a teacher,
What should it be?
I have a dream, a dream to travel the world.
I had a dream when I was 6,
I had a dream to be a fairy.
I had a dream to dance, I did,
I went to ballet when I was 6.
I'd love to see what it's like to be an animal,
To be a cat, to have a name like Socks or Dobby.
I'd love to be just like that.

Eliza Fairclough
The Queen Katherine School, Kendal

I Have A Dream . . .

A dream of riches, glitches and money,
I'd buy all the joke books and then I'd be funny.

I'd buy lots of books, loads of paper and pens,
Just if I had some money it really depends.

If I do well in school, try to follow the rules,
Oh I do hope, I do hope I do well in school.

Do well in exams to get a good job,
If I earn lots of money I never will rob.

I'd buy a new car, I could then travel really far,
I'd go to the salon, get my hair and nails done,
If I had the money I'd sit all day in the sun,
Buy a huge home, I'd not be alone.

I'd take with me my dog, give her a bed fit for a queen,
She'd be dressed the best that she's been.

I'd sing loads of songs so that people can dance,
Britney and J-Lo do not have a chance.

I have a dream of riches, glitches and money,
But I'm glad I have friends and my family,
You see, if I didn't have them, oh where would I be.

Jasmine Box (12)
The Queen Katherine School, Kendal

Nobody Cares

I have a dream, a dream that animals are treated
With love and kindness,
That they are cuddled and kissed
And shown that they have a home to live in happiness.

From China to America animals are mistreated,
When they should be allowed respect
And be treated as us fellow humans would be.
All suffer, young and old.

Our brothers and sisters are skinning, slaughtering
And murdering our domestic animals for *just* a bit of *fun.*
We cannot talk, accusing other countries of harming animals
As us ourselves are experimenting on innocent animals at this
very moment.

If this poem does not get through to you then just think,
What if it was the other way round and we were the victims.

Sarah Breeze (12)
The Queen Katherine School, Kendal

I Have A Dream

I have a dream, the world will be full of peace,
I have a dream, people will be treated equally,
I have a dream, no poverty will occur,
I have a dream, no war will disrupt the world,
I have a dream, no violence will be a problem,
I have a dream, to have no murder, slaughter
Or disturbance in homes across our lands,
I have a dream, for where there is no love,
Happiness or kindness, it will be filled with it,
I have a dream, a dream, a dream, a dream.

Lorna Bell (13)
The Queen Katherine School, Kendal

I Have A Dream

I have a dream
That I have seen
Children that are poor,
Water and food that is needed
As they sit there cold and sore,
Hoping that they get shelter,
Food, water and more.
That is what I want for the
children that are poor.
Killing and stabbing is not a good thing,
Beating up 2 year olds with bricks,
Fists, pushing and kicking
And breaking their wrists.
Silly little arguments grow into
Stupid large fights,
Going down alleyways,
Seeing the crime and watching
The bullying pass the time.
Battered and bruised, torn apart,
Why did this crime have to start?

Jayne Stephenson (13)
The Queen Katherine School, Kendal

A Dream

A dream is something inside your head,
That shows you what you want.
Some people's dreams will come true,
Some people's dreams will not.
Dreams in your sleep can be horrible,
They might not always go right.
Dreams can be full of sadness, pain, adrenaline, fright.

Children's dreams can often be good,
Killing dragons with ease,
But they can just as easily go wrong
And that dragon won't die in your dream.

A dream is unpredictable,
Can be good, bad or not true,
But every person is different
So your dream depends on you!

Sarah Knowles (12)
The Queen Katherine School, Kendal

Da Dream

I had a dream one night,
Don't worry, it did not give me a fright.
It was full of chocolate and sweets,
It was a real treat.
There were loads of furry yellow ducks,
No work, no school, no books!
It was perfect!

Sarah Harrison
The Queen Katherine School, Kendal

I Have A Dream

I have a dream,
A dream of dreams,
One with many different themes,
One was good,
One was bad,
One was really, really sad!

I have a dream,
A dream of dreams,
One with many different teams,
One was ace,
One was fast,
One was coming from the past!

Siena Townley (12)
The Queen Katherine School, Kendal

I Have A Dream

I had a dream
Although it seems
I was a rockstar
With my favourite pop star.

I was the lead singer
And my best mate was a pinger
All the fans cheered
But some were weird.

Soon I got very rich
And so was my twin,
From being on a football pitch
I soon got married to a footballer,
His brother was a tug of warrer.

Lauren Davidson
The Queen Katherine School, Kendal

Dreams

If dreams came true,
Then what would we do?
We could fly though the air
Or just stop, stand and stare.
Aspirations are dreams
And that's what it seems.
You could sit under the trees
And mess around when you please.
But you must always remember
Aspirations are dreams
And that's what it seems.

James Kalra
The Queen Katherine School, Kendal

I Have A Dream!

I had a dream just the other night,
It was alright but it gave me a fright.
It was about my grandma and me too,
I dreamt that she was really ill.
She was in hospital on a comfy bed,
But I still felt very sad and upset.
I was very afraid and worried too,
So I got up and went to the loo!
I got back in bed,
And cleared my head,
But my grandma died the next day!

Abbey Hunt (12)
The Queen Katherine School, Kendal

I Have A Dream

I dream of being a drummer in a rocking band,
I'd rock on night and day in every different land.
I'd lead the band with a beat,
With screaming fans on their feet.
I'd love it every night and day
And I'd also get extra pay.

Greg Nelson (11)
The Queen Katherine School, Kendal

I Have A Dream

I have a dream,
A dream that may come true.
I dream of being a footballer
For a team which I don't know who.

Maybe I'll be famous,
I'm not sure if I want to.
Yes, I want to be a footballer,
I'll stick to the team like glue.

And so this means
I'll try my best.
I won't give up when things get rough,
In proudness I'll wear their vest.

I want to be a striker
Or actually a goalkeeper.
Whatever it ends up to be
I don't want to be a defender.

Someday I want to be rich,
To be loaded with cash.
Although money isn't everything,
It buys your secret stash.

I also want to get married,
He might be a footballer too.
If he was a footballer,
We'd support each other all the way through!

Maybe I'll play for Leeds United,
The team I've supported since I was four.
That would be my dream,
But I would like to play for England more.

I have a dream,
A dream that may come true.
I dream of being a footballer,
For a team which I don't know who.

Steph Smith (12)
The Queen Katherine School, Kendal

Dreams, Dreams

Dreams, dreams,
In some dreams you can fly,
In some dreams you rule the world,
In some dreams you're the best,
Everybody dreams, how about you?

Dreams, dreams,
In some dreams there are monsters,
In some dreams you're the monster,
In some dreams there are witches,
Everybody dreams, how about you?

Dreams, dreams,
In my dreams nothing goes wrong,
In my dreams everybody's rich,
In my dreams nobody's poor,
I dream, how about you?

Matthew Bowler (12)
The Queen Katherine School, Kendal

England's My Dream

I had a dream one night,
It didn't give me a fright.
I met my star
Even though he lives far.
My hero is Steven Gerrard.
England is my dream,
The man who I would love to see.
My hero Steven Gerrard.

Amy Wilson (12)
The Queen Katherine School, Kendal

Dream

I wish, I wish everybody had the right to learn
And to go to school.
I wish they learnt English, maths, science,
Religious education, citizenship and sports.
I wish they had a good job
And a very good education.
I wish, I wish everybody was free of illness.
I wish everybody could walk.
I wish, I wish nobody would smoke again.

Chris Swift (11)
The Queen Katherine School, Kendal

I Wish

I wish, I wish,
I wish there was enough fish
For the people in poverty.

I wish, I wish,
I wish there was a way
To arrest the KKK.

I wish, I wish,
I wish there was no war
Because it fills the world with blood and gore.

I wish, I wish,
I wish there was enough water
So the people in poverty could have a son and daughter.

I wish, I wish,
I wish this could be true,
Before the day I become blue.

Nick Brennand
The Queen Katherine School, Kendal

Dreams!

I dream of all the people, animals and birds,
To be able to go and walk and fly without being hurt.
I dream of black and white to be free,
I dream for clean water for poor, sick and homeless.
I dream we could go to school,
Learn, play and laugh.
I dream no one would die through horrible deaths.
I dream all the wars would stop and settle nicely.
My biggest dream is the biggest of all,
I dream of peace,
I dream of a perfect world.

Jessica Marshall (11)
The Queen Katherine School, Kendal

I Have A Dream

I have a dream that arguments
which could lead to war
could be resolved, and then peace
would be flowing like a steady stream.

For the world we live in is split,
it is like a ball from space,
you can see the different expressions
on their faces.

Food is needed whether it has been
conjured by a magician or stabbed
on one's plate.

Education would neither go amiss,
whether it is steady,
the people of poverty are ready.

Shelter, some live in boxes,
Some if they could would live like foxes.

War breaks out, some kids go barmy,
some leave for the army.

Some kids are clever, some wish
they never had got into the school endeavour.

Our pride has been washed away
as quick as seaweed on a stormy day.

Please help us because my
dream is not mean, it is to be
put together like a puzzle -
Redefine the law of my way.

Tim Kieser (12)
The Queen Katherine School, Kendal

A Dream

I dream a dream that some day the war in Iraq will stop
And the KKK will lose the plot.
That poverty will really end
And the peace letter is ready to send.
I dream that suicide bombers will stop and think
Why turn the world a very dark pink.
I dream a dream.

Edward Rymell (11)
The Queen Katherine School, Kendal

Pollution Is A Problem

Pollution is a problem
That none of us can stop.
But at least we could try
To make pollution drop.

Think of generations
Down the line from us,
They will live in worry,
Learn to catch the bus.

Care for the environment,
Throw litter in the bin,
For what the world is doing
Is such a terrible sin.

Reuse all your paper,
Recycle every can,
For it is the worst crime
Ever committed by man.

The clouds up above
Stained the colour grey,
Let's lower greenhouse gases
Whatever you may say.

Frances Butcher (11)
The Queen Katherine School, Kendal

Dream For The World

I dream for the world
That everyone had food and water,
No guns,
No bombs,
Just peace for the world.

I dream for the world
That everyone has homes,
Enough freedom,
Enough medicine,
Just peace for the world.

I dream for the world
That people can just stand up for themselves,
Enough money
And clothes
For everyone to survive on.

I dream for the world
Not to split into two,
Half rich,
Half poor,
We should all play a part.

I dream for the world
That everyone should go to school,
Why should people lose out?
They should have a chance,
Everyone deserves a good education.

I dream for the world,
Leave animals alone,
Shouldn't they have a life
Just like us,
Shouldn't they be left alone.

Keeley Howson (12)
The Queen Katherine School, Kendal

I Have A Dream

I have a dream that war should be no more.
Give water to those in poverty,
They scavenge for food when the wealthy take food for granted.
Give money to the poor then poverty would be no more.

I dream that there would be no more war,
No one would be killed,
The world would be a better place,
No more pollution, make the world smell nicer and look nicer.

James Hicks (11)
The Queen Katherine School, Kendal

I Have A Dream

I have a dream that all countries would unite.
I have a dream that all the racism throughout the world
Would disappear and be erased from history.
I have a dream that every last person could have clean water
And a good food supply.
I have a dream that everyone would be equal in this world.
I have a dream that no cars would be belching out fumes
Of thick smoke and polluting the clean fresh air.
I have a dream that the world was a better and happier place.

Charlie MacKenzie (12)
The Queen Katherine School, Kendal

Dreams

I wish a dream
Of chocolate and cream.
When the stars are shining bright
I toss and turn onto my right.

I wish I had power to end war
As all this shooting is making me bored.
Just think of all those children
Who have no home, not even a den.

Why do we kill animals? The poor things,
We do it for greed, watches and rings.
People getting hit, punched and kicked,
They must hate getting picked.

Suddenly I wake up,
I have a drink out of my cup.
I hear my parents having a row,
Can't we sort all this right now!

Charlotte Harrison (11)
The Queen Katherine School, Kendal

The World

I have a dream
That the world will scream
And poverty will be gone.
People will no longer be sad
And homeless people will be glad.
Will poverty ever end
Or will we have to continue with this money bend?
I thank those people that faithfully died,
Just to keep our country's pride.
If we practise what we preach
The world will be better for us all.
I think those people that made a petulant speech
Will improve the world
Now we come to the end of my poem
I hope you will be sensitive and not commit a crime.

Jack Dawson
The Queen Katherine School, Kendal

Dreams I Have

I wish slaving and world hunger would stop.
Help stop kids from working and let them have an education like us.
People starving, when we have lots of food going to waste every day.
I wish dying would stop so that we can help,
Help those people who are dying in wars,
Dying of drought,
Dying from lack of food,
Dying of pollution,
Dying of global warming.
I wish that every person has an equal right to medicine,
Let those people who need medicine have it.
I wish racism would completely stop.
Everyone is equal to things in this world,
No matter what colour they are or what religion.
I wish the world was litter free,
Millions of animals die every year by getting trapped
In cans, glass and nets.
I wish the world would change to electric cars,
Too much pollution goes into the air every day by driving.
I wish people would talk instead of fighting,
Help stop these wars by talking.
I wish people would notice what's happening.
Ask yourself what you can do to help.

Laura McQuillan
The Queen Katherine School, Kendal

Poverty

Poverty is mad,
Poverty is sad,
We all hate poverty
Because it is bad.

Money for us all,
Mostly for the poor.
We all need money
But the poor need it more.

Charity needs money for the poor,
Give charity money more and more.

Luke Walsh
The Queen Katherine School, Kendal

I Had A Dream

I had a dream that I could
Change the world completely.
If poor people could have as much money
As professional players playing football.

And I wish I could make
Everybody have the same amount of money
And brilliant cars and a nice house to live in
With a full nice family.

I had a dream about that
Because I would like everybody
To be the same in different ways
Eg: everybody has a great life.

Jack Carradice (11)
The Queen Katherine School, Kendal

Clones

I have a dream
That people will be themselves
And not everyone else
And the air will be filled
With the meaningful flattering
Of total airheads
Who could do so much more.
I have a dream
That we will wear our clothes and hair
How we like, not how they like
And no one does what everyone else is doing,
Owning the smallest mobile,
Owning the clothes you only buy for the price tag.
I have a dream
That intelligence will come
Before looking good
And impressing that boy (or girl)
And people still enjoy songs
Once they've left the charts.
I have a dream
That people will have ambition
And stand out
And not scorn those who have the courage
To be their own person
And never mind poverty!
Focus on life's big question,
Is my hair still in place?

Ciara Houghton
The Queen Katherine School, Kendal

I Have A Dream!

The average dream
Is filled with ice cream,
Nice and cold
With lots of gold,
That is the average dream,
But imagine a world without water!
The supply is getting shorter!
Especially in countries like Africa,
Soon there will be no more laughter,
So turn the water off when you brush your teeth
To save the water stored beneath.
So don't have a bath, have a shower,
If you want to save the world.
You have the power!

Ben Butcher (12)
The Queen Katherine School, Kendal

I Have A Dream

We want world peace,
To end suffering,
So the world can stand up and sing,
United together,
World peace forever,
For we are all equal and special,
This world is real,
We are lucky,
Help the world you and me,
Black and white,
If we both act right,
We get rid of racism,
Thanks to Martin Luther King and Nelson Mandela,
Legends forever,
They stood up,
Said what they had to say,
Changed the world from racism,
Racism was banned,
It was what they had planned,
Martin Luther King had a dream,
That he did not like racism it did seem,
About equal rights,
So that they could sit in the same restaurants at nights,
He got put in prison for what he believed in,
For he was the peace king,
His speeches were good,
For he wasn't a gangster in a hood,
He was black not white,
His speeches were good and he was incredibly bright.

Alex Stewart (11)
The Queen Katherine School, Kendal

Dreams

I have a dream!
I have a dream which will help.
I have a dream and it may come true.
I have a dream that could save you.
This dream is to stop poverty in this world.
I have a dream just like him,
His dream came true and he died trying too.
Bang, bang, bang, bang, he was dead,
Lying there as he bled.
Please help stop world poverty
For me, for you.

Lois Archer (13)
The Queen Katherine School, Kendal

I Have A Dream

I hate poverty,
Poverty is bad,
I hate poverty because it makes me sad.

Money from me and my dad,
Will end poverty then I
Will not be sad.

People in poverty
Don't have bags,
Instead they have rags.

Josh Wallace (12)
The Queen Katherine School, Kendal

I Have A Dream

He had a dream,
A dream of world peace,
Then all he got was a prison sentence,
Soon after released,
A blow to the head,
Left his dreams shattered,
He had a dream,
Gone.

I have a dream,
A dream of a cure,
A cure for cancer,
To save people's lives,
I have a dream,
Possible.

Dreams can come true,
All you need is willpower,
Help and your friends,
It is all you need,
Dreams.

Kate Brennan
The Queen Katherine School, Kendal

I Have A Dream

I have a dream, a perfect life,
A lovely house,
All the money in the world,
A monkey and a swimming pool,
A footballer's wife is what I want to be,
I want to own a soft-top car
And loads and loads of clothes,
I want an island just for me
And a life eternity,
I have a dream.

I have a dream of world wide peace,
To end all depression,
I want black and white to live together,
In one large community,
I want to end global warming,
And stop all terrorists,
I want all people in the world
To live as equals, as one,
I have a dream.

Francesca Ward (12)
The Queen Katherine School, Kendal

I Dream

I dream that people can fly, instead of polluting with cars.
I dream world poverty is a joke and crime doesn't exist.
I dream of world peace and no global warming.
I dream people have rights to be treated the same.
I dream that trees can stop crying
And we can make paper out of something else.
I dream that animals aren't endangered
And tigers can be free like us.
I dream there are no nightmares and kids can stop screaming.
I dream that we don't die and can live together forever.
I dream all of these and I can dream many more.

Megan Holliday
The Queen Katherine School, Kendal

I Have A Dream

My dream is a dream that is personal to me,
It's bundled with animals for everyone to see.

A house in the country with acres of land,
For a lot of houses but some sand.

Cows and pigs and lots of dogs too,
A mansion filled with joy for me and you.

An animal shelter I will build,
Puppies and cats it would be filled.

As long as I had my animals with me
I would always be as happy as can be.

Lauren Bowness (12)
The Queen Katherine School, Kendal

I Have A Dream

I have a dream that nobody knows,
A dream of mine is to own a dog's home
With dogs of all shapes and sizes.

I have a dream of having a horse
With the mane as silky as snow.

Jade Stanworth (12)
The Queen Katherine School, Kendal

My Dream

I had a dream last night,
It was very strange,
I dreamt of a kite
High out of range,
Gliding through the sky,
Colours shining in the night,
I do not lie,
But the kite had a fight,
With a tree that is,
Banging and crashing of wood,
It fluttered lifelessly to the ground,
I thought this is not very good
So I picked up my kite with one hand
And took it back home,
Out of the sand.
A few weeks later
I have to say
It was gliding again
Across the bay.

Freya Brodie-Stedman (12)
The Queen Katherine School, Kendal

I Have A Dream

I dream for . . .
The end of poverty,
For there to be no rich or poor but all to be equal.

I dream that . . .
Richer countries will stop making poor countries
Depend on them in times of need,
But teach them to think for themselves.

I dream that . . .
Everyone will be able to understand each other,
To help each other and care for each other.

What is the point of having lots of money,
If you don't help those with less?

Charlotte Dowker (12)
The Queen Katherine School, Kendal

My Wish Is To Not Let This Happen

Can you hear the wind
Whistling through the trees,
The leaves rustling gently
And the sticky sap rolling down the trunk?

Can you see the birds
Gliding on a summer's day,
The fox cubs frolicking in a field,
And the badgers meandering through their forest?

Their forest, the very same one
People have been felling trees earlier that day.

Go back six months later
And where will the badgers be?
The fox cubs, the birds,
The sounds, the smells, the sights,
Dead? Homeless? Gone?

Now that my poem is complete,
Let my wishes the people meet.

Freya Blyth (12)
The Queen Katherine School, Kendal

I Have A Dream

I have a dream to be a professional footballer.
I have a dream to be on top of the world.
I have a dream to lift the European Cup.
I have a dream to lift the World Cup.

I have a dream to be the best.
I have a dream to captain Liverpool and England.
I have a dream to be chanted at by the crowd.
I have a dream to take that chance now.

I have a dream to score the goals.
I have a dream to raise everybody's goals.
I have a dream to play for Liverpool,
Then those thugs who doubted me would be such fools.

I have a dream to make these fans scream.
I have a dream to have that dream.
I have a dream to be famous all around,
But before all that I need to be *found*.

Stephen Looker (12)
The Queen Katherine School, Kendal

I Have A Dream

My dream is as good as yours,
Maybe even better.
I wish I had paws
And four legs
Or hooves and a mane,
Cute pet names
And freedom to do what I want.
I want to run all day,
I wish all day I could play.
I really wish I was an animal,
Full of energy and could be
Cuddled all day and when the children
Get home I would play even more.
I wish I had a fluffy bobtail
Or long bouncy legs,
Hooves that clatter,
Paws that tatter,
That's what I want in every matter.
I want, I wish
I was a fish.
To swim all day in and out of the Titanic,
But all the sharks will eat me.

Georgia Davis (11)
The Queen Katherine School, Kendal

Global Warming

What causes global warming?
Carbon dioxide and greenhouse gases,
Heat up the world like magnifying glasses.
Fuel from fires go up in smoke,
So if you swallow you start to choke,

What are the effects of global warming?
Melting ice caps in the Arctic,
Because of the sun, time starts to tick.
Rivers dry up so crops don't grow,
Famine and thirst invade, *oh no!*

What are the other effects of global warming?
Rivers overflow and streams flood,
Destroying lives and filled with blood.
Animals' environment changes all the time,
All this is our fault, it's a terrible crime.

Emma Haddon (12)
The Queen Katherine School, Kendal

I Have A Dream

What's wrong with this world?
There is so much hate
Why do people bomb and kill?
Why do they hurt so many innocent lives?
Children without mothers,
Mothers without brothers.
Who cares if you're black or white?
Who cares if you're dim or bright?
Who cares if you're a Jew or a Sikh?
Who cares if you're Muslim or Christian?
People believe in different things.
Why not? What's wrong with that?
There is so much hate everywhere you look.
Why can't people believe different things
And still live in peace, together as one.
Don't try to change people,
Let them be who they are
Whether you understand it or not.
Believe what you believe
And let others do the same.

Helena Shorrock (12)
The Queen Katherine School, Kendal

I Have A Dream

My dream is for world peace.
No destruction and no wars
But there are people in the world
Who won't keep to this.
I have a dream,
That gets ripped apart at the seams.
In Africa there are children dying,
There are families dead and no one crying.
People suffer every day,
And we should try and help them in any way.
So as you can tell my dream is for world peace,
Not destruction or war in the streets.
I have a dream.

Rachael Wild (12)
The Queen Katherine School, Kendal

I Have A Dream

My dream is to be the best footballer in the world.
To be better than Ronaldinho at skills
And to tackle every football player in the world
And score past the best keeper in the world.
My dream is to make my own team
With me, Ronaldinho, Zinedine Zidane, Rooney
                                    and Van Nistelrooy.
My dream is to make lots of money and be famous
                                    all around the world.

Liam Esty (12)
The Queen Katherine School, Kendal

I Have A Dream

I have a dream

H ow my plan will work I don't know
A very hard plan it is
V is for victory of my plan
E veryone should listen

A t my plan

D o not kill
R ight the wrongs
E veryone unite
A nd fight as one
M any people fight for freedom

I f everyone could see
T he wrongs in this world

C are for the Earth
O h no I can't be bothered, is not allowed
U nder the skin is where you should look
L ots of people make a difference
D irty and polluted the Earth will get

W ork hard
O f all the polluted worlds we will pollute
R ight now our Earth is dying
K nowing how to stop this we must learn.

Sam Williamson
The Queen Katherine School, Kendal

I Have A Dream

I have a dream for all the world to come to peace.
I have a dream for Iraq to settle and come to peace.
I have a dream for all the killing to stop.
I have a dream for all the cars to not pollute.
I have a dream to be and do everything right again.
I have a dream and I wish this dream to come true.

Michael Akrigg
The Queen Katherine School, Kendal

I Have A Dream

I have a dream
That the future before me
Can be of peace and happiness
Not suffering crawling.

A mist of death covers this land
It may release itself
Like an uncurling band.

I have a dream of a world without hunger
No suffering or starving
Because they won't get younger.

So the message in this I'm trying to give
Is the future for once
Is not down to the kids.

Adam Simpson (13)
The Queen Katherine School, Kendal

I Have A Dream!

H appy, the world will be, if we help and give money.
E very day people die, ill and dry.
L iving and breathing they just manage to do
P lanning, they just can't do. If we help they will be able to.

I have a dream just like you!

Ellie Pearson
The Queen Katherine School, Kendal

I Have A Dream

Life goes on
With dreams in my pocket
Having everybody singing,
Let the fools that I used to know, go . . .
Don't let them look at me up and down from head to toe!

Dream
Love never ends
Dream
You love someone
Dream
You get that person
Dream
You get what you want
Dream
Life goes on!

Bianca Ford (14)
West Hatch High School, Chigwell

I Have A Dream

I have a dream
That everyone will get along.
I have a dream
That nobody does anything wrong.

I have a dream
That children will make a difference
And that our voices will be heard.
That more people will stand out
Instead of fitting in.
That people will stop following trends
And instead stand up and lead for what they think is right
But that will probably never happen.
I remember, this is only a dream
So I might as well forget it.

I used to have a dream
That everyone would get along
But now I have a nightmare
Where everyone is doing wrong.

Lauren Osborne (14)
West Hatch High School, Chigwell

I Have A Dream

I have a dream to make the world peaceful,
To stop all suffering and pain.

Our world is a dirty place, people commit crime
Quick clean our world, we're running out of time.

People rape, people hurt,
People treat you like you're dirt.

I have a dream to make the world peaceful,
To stop all suffering and pain.

People bully, people hit.
Gosh this world is really the pits.

People lie, people cheat,
Please don't treat us like this.

I have a dream to show the world, I'm going to accomplish this,
But will our world come together and bring this happiness?

Babita Parmar (14)
West Hatch High School, Chigwell

Question

An answer to a question.
A question to an answer.
If I question my answer,
Do I question my question?
If I question my question,
Do I question all purpose?
If all purpose is questioned,
How can I question
The answer to my question?
My dream is the answer,
The answer to my question.

Alex Gregory (14)
West Hatch High School, Chigwell

I Have A Dream

I have a dream
That there's no rich or poor.
I have a dream
We can open the door
To love and peace
Without the war.

I have a dream
That there is equality
A world with no pain
And a life full of quality.

I have a dream
That bullies are banished
That there is no fear
And no one feels famished.

I have a dream
Racism doesn't exist
And everyone feels happy to live
But why should they
When in the world we live
All we can do is take and not give?

Josie Wyre (14)
West Hatch High School, Chigwell

My Poem

I have a dream,
That one day basketball will be my life.
To feel the crowd's chants and to see the cheerleaders dance,
I want my adrenaline pumping whilst I do my dunking,
I want my family to be proud and my fans cheering loud,
I must fly like Michael and be as deadly as an icicle,
I've gotta shoot from downtown to be the best around,
I must beat the rest to be the best,
I dream of playing for Miami Heat with the best pair of sneakers
on my feet,
Why go shopping at the mall, when you could be playing basketball.

I may be fouled, to the line I go, players line up for my free throw,
I used to practise forever in my yard, kids used to think that I was
a retard,
All the times I dreamt of winning, I wish I could see myself now smiling
and grinning,
Cameras flash as I lift off my feet, I use the talent I earned off the street,
I'm capable of more it's so hard to believe, some say I'm one of the
next '23',
I grab my jersey and my shoes, when I go to a game, I believe I will
not lose,
When you walk through the gym door and out on the floor, you know
you want more,
I love the sound of shoes on the wooden floor but to think of training
it's so hard core,
Why be on the couch being lazy because if you don't play basketball
you are crazy.

Jordan Berry (14)
West Hatch High School, Chigwell

My Wish

I wish the world was all OK,
I wish for the homeless when I pray.

I wish the planet wasn't at war,
I wish we all loved as before.

I wish that bullying never happened on Earth,
I wish for no cruelty from London to Perth.

I wish the desert could get some rain,
I wish the killers could feel some pain.

I wish that one day my wish will come true,
My wish for the world, for me and for you.

Becky Hewitt (14)
West Hatch High School, Chigwell

If I Was God

If I had a dream,
It would be,
For everyone
To worship me.

I'd be king,
I'd be on top,
I'd give the people
I hate the chop.

If I ruled
There'd be no wars,
No terrorists,
No bombs
There'd be no flaws.

If I had the world in my hands,
I would destroy the terrorists' plans,
To bomb the world and prove they're right
If I was God for a single night.

Robert Mehmet (14)
West Hatch High School, Chigwell

I Have A Dream

I have a dream
To change children's lives
Make them enjoy their school time
To stop all the bullies
Make them understand fully
That what they are doing is wrong.

I have a dream
That everyone will get along
No abuse and rape
Or anything wrong
To clean up all the streets
Stop the crimes
Make a new world, introduce new times.

I have a dream
That everyone will have fun
All religions and races
Will come together as one
Love and world peace
Should be all we can see.

Alex Elliott (14)
West Hatch High School, Chigwell

My Dream To Be Different

Different,
Never the same,
That means unique,
You'll feel no pain.

Different,
Stand out,
Don't shadow,
Don't doubt.

Different,
Be yourself,
Be the only you
And no one else.

Different,
What people think, don't care
You live once
Do and dare.

Different.

Gemma Moulton (13)
West Hatch High School, Chigwell

I Have A Dream

I have a dream that kids rule the world and everybody has their way,
I have a thought that peace rules the world and everyone has their say.

I wish that hate was a crime and people only cared,
I hope that love is our rhyme and you are always there.

Life would be better if everyone could stand tall,
Life would be better if we could understand it all
and . . .
People would be kinder if we listened to their words,
People would be nicer if we acted more like birds
because . . .
We are all free spirits inside and everyone can see
That we are all alive inside, so see what you can achieve.

Lucy Hearn (13)
West Hatch High School, Chigwell

Peace

No more fighting,
No more war,
Peace in the world,
That's what we're all for.

Kick out racism,
Poverty too,
How would you feel,
If it happened to you.

Rich or poor,
Young or old,
Warm and safe,
To have and to hold.

The world would be,
My favourite place,
No matter your religion.
No matter your race.

I had a dream,
The strife was over,
Peace in the world
For ever and ever.

Rebekah Birch (13)
West Hatch High School, Chigwell

I Have A Dream

I have a dream,
That is full of world peace,
Where no fighting exists,
And all war has ceased.

I have a dream,
That all handbags are free,
In every shop,
From Gucci to Burberry.

I have a dream,
That nobody starved,
In all the poor countries,
So everyone laughed.

I have a dream,
Where everyone's equal,
Everyone's nice,
Nobody's evil.

I have a dream
Where everyone's good,
Where everyone's happy,
Like everyone should.

Hannah Bates (14)
West Hatch High School, Chigwell

I Have A Dream

I have a dream to change the world,
Stop smoking, drugs and crime,
Make everybody happy
And clean up all the grime.

So many people are in the wrong
And soon it needs to stop.
I have a dream to make things right
So bad issues are on top.

People hit and people steal
How do you think this makes me feel?
Worried, confused and shy,
Do you know how much abuse goes by?

Some people are cheating life
And taking it too far
We need to show we are in control
We've gone well over par.

Jessica Moores (14)
West Hatch High School, Chigwell

My Dreams

To d ream in the clouds
    T r avel the sky
Chang e the world
To be a n accountant
    m ix and match with life
Dream s.

Rebecca Wells (12)
West Hatch High School, Chigwell

I Wish . . .

The day my nan was diagnosed with cancer,
I felt angry and sad,
To know there was no cure and
Nothing I could do.
To see her wither like a flower, day by day.
I wish, I wish I didn't have to go through the torture
Of seeing her melt away,
Day by day.

Stephanie Leszman (12)
West Hatch High School, Chigwell

It's My Dream

My dream is not a dream I dream at night;
in bed;
eyes shut,
quiet.

It's what I feel,
It's what I think,
It's my hope,
It's my *dream*.

I dream happiness for my mother
for there's no other like my mother.

I dream a court,
I dream a judge,
I dream of me being a lawyer.

I dream blue skies,
I dream clean air,
I dream no more pollution.

I dream no more knives,
I dream no more guns,
I dream there is a solution.

My dream is not a dream I dream at night;
in bed;
eyes shut;
quiet.

It's what I think,
It's what I feel,
It's my hope,
It's my dream.

Laura Thompson (12)
West Hatch High School, Chigwell

I Have A Dream

Life is a terror, why can't we be merrier?
Life is a huge war, why do we treat the poor differently?
Life is a wicked thing broken into millions of pieces.
Life is a huge time bomb ready to explode.
Earth is a bubble, if you treat it badly it will pop!
I wish, the world was one.
I wish people were equal,
I wish money wasn't a big thing for people,
I wish that people who are not wealthy were part of a community
               where we were together,
I wish that dreams were real and true,
I wish that everything was fair and everything I wished for
                  came true.

I wish, I wish, I wish.

Bethan Howlett (12)
West Hatch High School, Chigwell

My Dream

I have a dream,
Which may not seem
Like every girl's dream.

They dream of tans,
They dream of boys,
But I simply dream of playing at Lords!

And the commentary man may say:
'Haripaul does it again for England!
They've won the Ashes!'

People say it's a boys' sport,
But I don't think that's a fair report!
I don't wanna play on a tennis court
I don't wanna play netball cos it's always my fault!

I just wanna play cricket
That's the end of that!
I *never* wanna let go of my cricket bat!

Tara Haripaul (12)
West Hatch High School, Chigwell

Perfection

An icon of perfection,
Or so that's what they're called.
We try to become our idols
Until the day we fall.

Why live as a copy
Of what's already been done
When do we let our hair down
And try to have some fun.

Fitting in isn't worth it,
If this is what we have to do,
Lining up like cattle
Why don't we try something new.

Our dreams of perfection,
Have come crashing down,
Her beauty's not so flawless
She's nothing without her crown.

Shauna Carroll (12)
West Hatch High School, Chigwell

I Have A Dream

I can change the world.

H ave the end of disease and hunger.
A ll the world happy.
V eterans treated with respect.
E verybody has a home.

A ll the world stops fighting.

D ream for a billion happy smiles.
R eaching for their goals.
E veryone is equal.
A ll can change if they try.
M aybe this could happen, a dream to aspire to.

Eddie Pickup & Rhys Corderoy (12)
West Hatch High School, Chigwell

I Have A Dream

I have a dream,
A dream without hate.

I have a dream,
A dream without bullying.

I have a dream,
A dream without weapons.

I have a dream,
A dream without terrorism.

I have a dream,
A dream without racism.

I have a dream,
A dream without war.

I have a dream,
A dream without murder.

I have a dream,
A dream without drug addicts.

I have a dream,
A dream without alcoholics.

I have a dream,
A dream without criminals.

I have a dream,
A dream without all of the bad things in the world.

I have a dream.

Stephen Farrugia (14)
West Hatch High School, Chigwell

I Have A Dream

Sitting in a dressing room going over my words;
looking at the clock and listening to the birds.
The butterflies in my stomach are flying round and round;
I listen out carefully but cannot hear a sound.
Bang! Bang! goes the door as I quickly stand;
and take the mic from the table and put it in my hand.
I take a deep breath and pull open the door;
as I begin to feel sick more and more.
As I pace backstage looking all around;
watching all the people as my heart pounds.
As I climb the stairs to the stage;
the adrenaline rushes through me like an animal let out of a cage.
As I start to walk my legs feel numb;
I close my eyes and think, *this is for you mum.*
The lights dim and the curtain slowly rises;
as the spotlight beams down, the music starts with no surprises.
I wait for my note then start to sing;
as I look upon the audience, one million people screaming.
A passionate vibe runs up my spine;
this is one the most memorable moments in time.
I don't want this feeling to ever end;
I have my fans, family and all my friends.
The music in the background fades;
as I sing the last word on the page.
The audience roars standing on the floor;
my name is screamed from door to door.
I thank my fans and wish them a safe journey home;
the light goes off I am all alone.
I go backstage and into my mirror I say;
'I told you this girl would always find her way!'

Lucy-Jay Fox (14)
West Hatch High School, Chigwell

I Have A Dream

I have a dream
that I can rule the world
where people will obey me and do as I say.
It will be a lot like a computer game
where you control the people and make them do what
you want them to do.
What a dream that would be.

I have a dream
that I can play football.
People watching me play, everyone knowing my name
and the best feeling will be scoring a goal
and being able to celebrate like Wayne Rooney or Ronaldinho.
What a dream that could be.

I have a dream
that I can be a successful person
having a good job, nice house and a family.
Being a grown-up will be a great adventure,
driving a car, watching films and being able to do things freely.
What a life that would be.

Ashley White (14)
West Hatch High School, Chigwell

My World

When I look at the world today
I know I should use my voice and say
That this world could be a better place
All you need is a lovely smile on your face
I dream of a world without any crime
I wish for a world with no sorrow or devastation
Where everyone smiles and shows appreciation
I dream of a world without any pollution
This will help the world's evolution
I wish for a world with no war but celebration
This is what I wish for my generation.

Emily Phillips (12)
West Hatch High School, Chigwell

Goodbye Mum

I know that you are happy up there in Heaven,
I know you look down on me
And see me
But I don't see you anymore.
I wish I could hug you
And kiss you
But I can't anymore.

It was hard
For me, saying goodbye to you,
You were the one
Who made me laugh
And you made me embarrassed.
But now you make me cry
At night I wish you were in my arms
And I pray
For you to be back again.

It is hard for me now,
I don't see you,
But you will always be in my heart
Forever and ever.

Cameron Green (12)
Windsor School, Germany

I Love You

You are the sparkle in my eye
You are the smile on my lips
You are the chuckle in my laugh
You are the beat in my heart
You are the blossom in my life
You are my forever
I love you
xxx

Rebecca Roberts (12)
Windsor School, Germany

I Love

You are the spar...
You are the smi...
You are the chuckle... light
You are the beat...
You are the blossom... my life
You are my...
I love you
xxx

Rebecca Nob... (10)
Windsor School, Oxf...